SANDY'S CIRCUS

A STORY ABOUT ALEXANDER CALDER

BY TANYA LEE STONE   ILLUSTRATED BY BORIS KULIKOV

VIKING

VIKING

Published by Penguin Group

Penguin Young Readers Group, 345 Hudson Street, New York, New York 10014, U.S.A.

Penguin Group (Canada), 90 Eglinton Avenue East, Suite 700, Toronto, Ontario, Canada M4P 2Y3

(a division of Pearson Penguin Canada Inc.)

Penguin Books Ltd, 80 Strand, London WC2R 0RL, England

Penguin Ireland, 25 St Stephen's Green, Dublin 2, Ireland (a division of Penguin Books Ltd)

Penguin Group (Australia), 250 Camberwell Road, Camberwell, Victoria 3124, Australia

(a division of Pearson Australia Group Pty Ltd)

Penguin Books India Pvt Ltd, 11 Community Centre, Panchsheel Park, New Delhi – 110 017, India

Penguin Group (NZ), 67 Apollo Drive, Rosedale, North Shore 0632, New Zealand

(a division of Pearson New Zealand Ltd)

Penguin Books (South Africa) (Pty) Ltd, 24 Sturdee Avenue, Rosebank, Johannesburg 2196, South Africa

Penguin Books Ltd, Registered Offices: 80 Strand, London WC2R 0RL, England

First published in 2008 by Viking, a division of Penguin Young Readers Group

10 9 8 7 6 5 4 3 2 1

Photograph on page 37 copyright © André Kertész, 1929.

Reproduced by permission of The Estate of André Kertész/Higher Pictures

LIBRARY OF CONGRESS CATALOGING-IN-PUBLICATION DATA

Stone, Tanya Lee.

Sandy's circus : a story about Alexander Calder / by Tanya Lee Stone ; illustrated by Boris Kulikov.

p. cm.

Includes bibliographical references.

ISBN 978-0-670-06268-3 (hardcover)

1. Calder, Alexander, 1898-1976—Juvenile literature. 2. Circus in art—Juvenile literature. I. Kulikov,

Boris. II. Title.

NB237.C28S75 2008

730.92—dc22

2008008380

Manufactured in China   Set in P22 Parrish Roman   Book design by Jim Hoover

FOR JAKE AND LIZA. AND FOR EVERYONE BRAVE ENOUGH
TO FOLLOW THEIR OWN UNIQUE PATH IN LIFE. —TLS

TO NATALIE B.   —BK

THERE ONCE WAS an artist named Alexander Calder.
Only he didn't call himself Alexander. And he didn't call
the things he made art.

Everyone called him Sandy. He had been making his objects
since he was a kid. Sandy's mother was a painter. His father
was a sculptor. Even though they moved from Pennsylvania
to Arizona to California to New York and back to California,
his parents always made sure Sandy had a workshop and tools.

He made his friends toys and jewelry from scraps of wood, leather, and wire he would pick up off the street. Sandy built his sister Peggy a castle for her doll—complete with a moat! He and Peggy made toy animals and played circus in the workshop.

Even though Sandy loved creating things, he didn't always want to be an artist. He went to college and learned more about making things by studying to be an engineer. Sandy had different jobs but never really liked any of them.

Then he worked as a fireman in the boiler room of a ship. One night, he was sleeping up on deck, sailing between San Francisco and New York. When he woke, he was awestruck. On one side of the ship was "a fiery red sunrise." On the other, the full moon shone "like a silver coin." The sight made Sandy want to go to art school, and he did.

Artists need to work. A newspaper hired Sandy to draw the Ringling Brothers and Barnum & Bailey circus. For two weeks, day and night, he went to the stadium, drawing as many different parts of the circus as he could.

He loved sketching the elephants, the flying trapeze, the lion tamer, and the dancers. Sandy sat in different parts of the theater to see from up high, down low, off to the side.

The next year, 1926, he decided to go to Paris. Why Paris? Because that city was alive with art. And Sandy said, "In Paris it's a compliment to be called crazy." Sandy rode through the streets of Paris on his orange bicycle. He carried a roll of wire around his shoulder and a pair of pliers in his pocket.

When Sandy bumped into a friend, out came the wire and pliers. He would twist and bend and curl while he chatted. And before they said *adieu*, Sandy would give his friend a gift—*voilà!* A small portrait of the person—made of wire.

One day, Sandy made a little wire lion. He built a colorful cage
for the lion. Of course, since the lion was a wild animal, it needed
a tamer. So Sandy made him, too.

Then he made high-wire walkers and a high wire for them to
walk on. And a safety net, in case they should fall.

And a flying trapeze.

And a red stage.

Sandy started to see a whole circus come to life before his eyes.

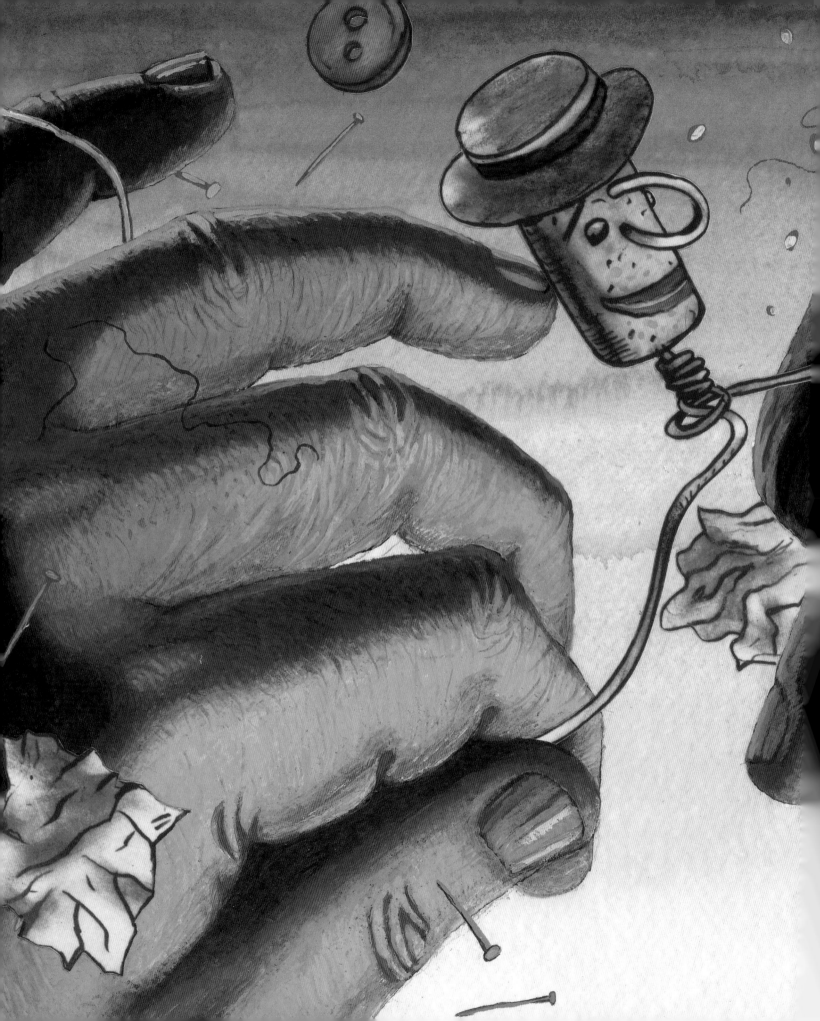

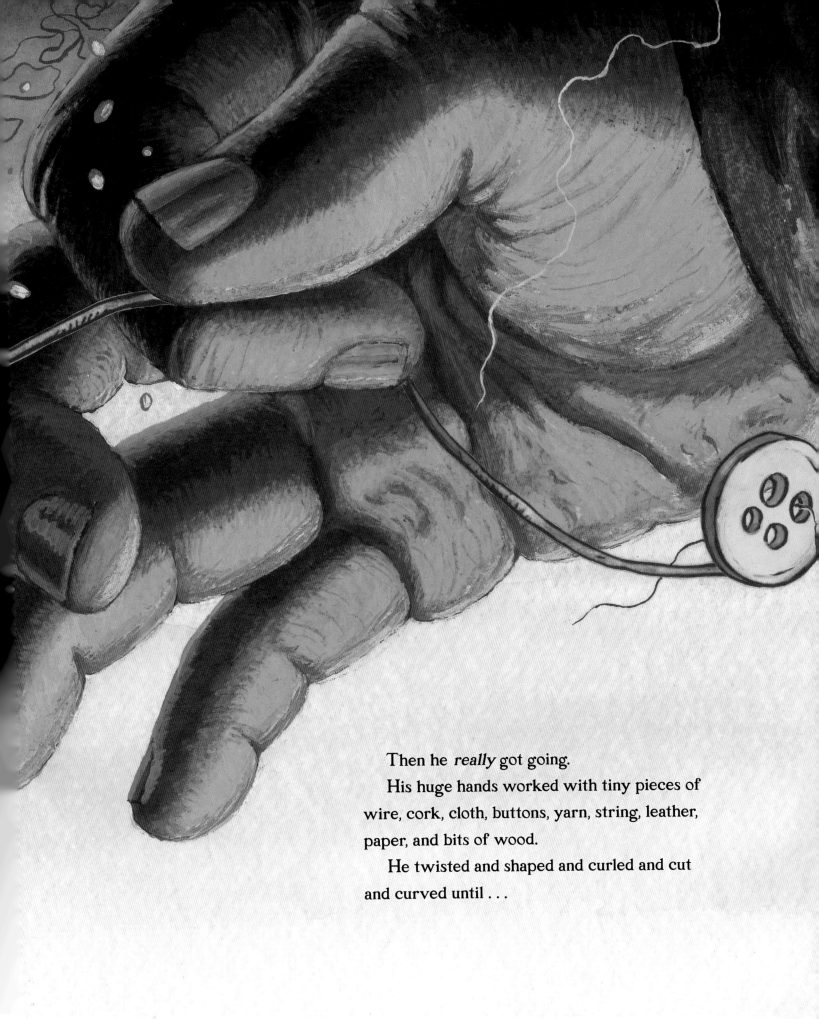

Then he *really* got going.

His huge hands worked with tiny pieces of wire, cork, cloth, buttons, yarn, string, leather, paper, and bits of wood.

He twisted and shaped and curled and cut and curved until . . .

Sandy was ready to put on a big-top circus show!

His circus filled two suitcases. *Click. Click.* Sandy set up the stage with his animals and performers wherever and whenever he could.

He went back and forth, back and forth, from Paris to New York—those suitcases always along for the ride. During one stay in New York, Sandy made more animals and acrobats. His circus grew to fill five suitcases. When it was showtime, out came the suitcases. *Click. Click. Click. Click. Click.*

A friend wound up the gramophone to start the music. Sandy boomed a greeting to his audience in the voice of his wire ringmaster Monsieur Loyal, announcing the performance was about to begin. On his knees, this bear of a man worked the springs and strings and levers of his clever creations, making them leap, run, and dance.

Hear the whistle blow!

Horns blare!

See the Flying Flippolinis flip.

The lion roars!

The lion tamer tames.

Seals bark, tossing a ball from nose to nose.

Rigoulot, the strong man, bends to his toes and raises a huge barbell high above his head, showing off for his beloved Bearded Lady.

Horses gallop.

Birds flutter.

Dogs dance on whirly, twirly legs.

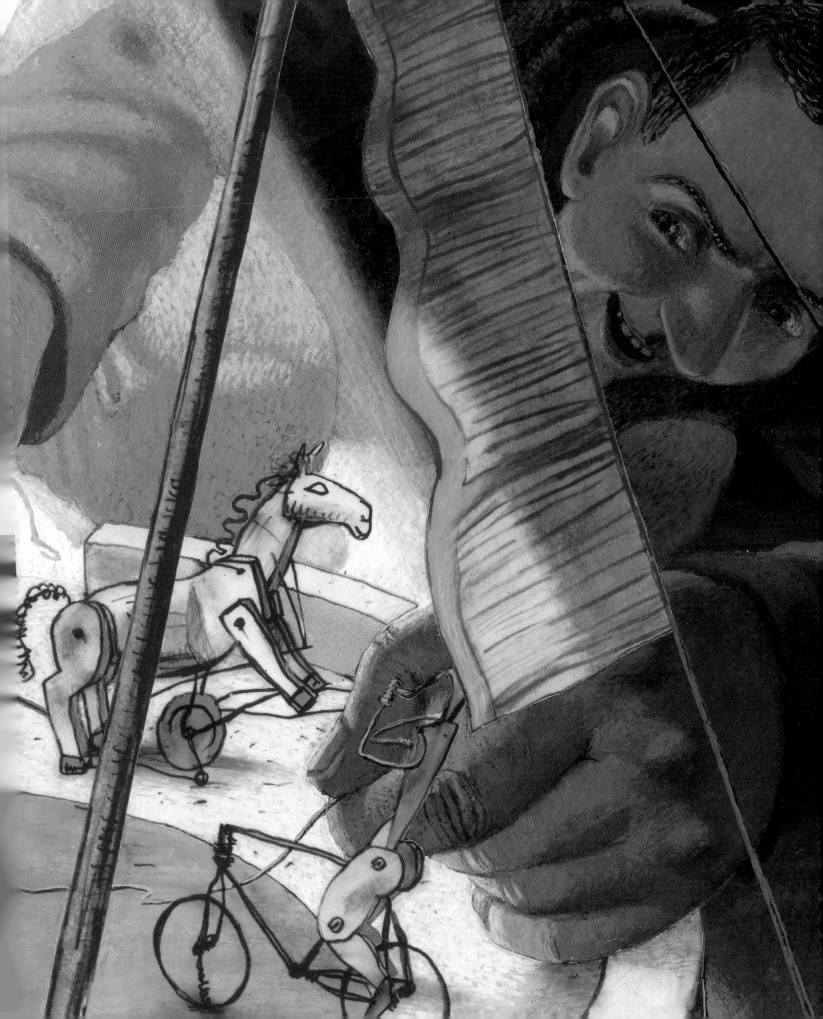

Cativo the Clown plays tricks on his fellow performers. He dangerously distracts the ax-thrower just as he hurls his ax at the wire girl. Oh, no! Injury under the Big Top! But never fear—help is on the way! Sirens wail. Two wire rescue workers race in to carry the girl off on a teeny-tiny stretcher.

Sometimes the show went on for hours. There were chariot races and bucking broncos. A belly dancer, camel, and kangaroo. Sandy crawled around on his hands and knees, arranging his wire animals and circus folk, setting them in motion to perform for the crowd. After the grand finale, he brought them all back for a bow.

Encore! Encore! The crowd laughed and clapped and cheered for more!

Word spread throughout Paris and New York. Everyone wanted
to see Sandy's circus. They loved how "full of joy and fun" it was.
They loved how Sandy's work was "always in motion."

People said:

"He has discovered, in playing, a new world."

His art "has the force of the ocean."

Sandy delighted in crafting things that moved. He made
new kinds of art, hanging his shapes up, connecting pieces
to each other with wire, and letting the air drift and spin
them into motion. In doing so, he turned ordinary objects into
extraordinary art, and invented the very first mobiles.
And it all started with Sandy's magical, moveable circus.

AUTHOR'S NOTE

ALEXANDER CALDER was one of the most important American artists of the twentieth century, and his circus was one of his most important works. I remember the first time I saw Alexander Calder's work outside of a museum. My soon-to-be husband and I were enjoying a lazy Sunday drive in the western hills of Connecticut. As if by magic, in the midst of cows and serene country roads, a large yard appeared, filled with bright, bold sculptures. The line, color, and joyousness of these structures were unmistakable to me. "Stop the car!"

We climbed out and peered—as politely as possible—into the backyard. Okay, we stared incredulously. I had no idea that Calder had lived in Roxbury, Connecticut. But it quickly dawned on us that we were standing on the edge of the Calder estate. It was easy to imagine what life might have been like in that backyard when Sandy Calder was alive, passing out croquet mallets to friends who dropped by and sharing his love of life with all who were lucky enough to know him.

Ever since that moment, I have wanted to capture a piece of the Calder essence in a story. The man *invented* the mobile—a whimsical sculpture artfully designed to move as freely as the air or wind lets it. It's a form we now take for granted, yet even the mobiles that hang over baby cribs would not exist without Calder. He also built enormous, bold metal sculptures that stood still, called stabiles. I hope I have been able to convey some of the Calder magic through the story of Sandy's Circus.

Right: Famed Hungarian photographer André Kertész took this photo of Calder performing his circus in Paris, circa 1929.

 # SOURCES USED

Calder, Alexander. *An Autobiography with Pictures.* New York: Pantheon, 1966.

_____. *Calder Creatures Great and Small.* New York, Dutton, 1985.

Lipman, Jean. *Calder's Universe.* New York: Viking, 1976.

Rower, Alexander S. C. *Calder Sculpture.* Washington, D.C.: National Gallery of Art, 1998.

Smithsonian Archives of American Art. "Oral History Interview with Alexander Calder at Perls Gallery." October 26, 1971. Interviewer: Paul Cummings.

Sweeney, James Johnson. *Alexander Calder.* New York: The Museum of Modern Art, 1943.

Wilkin, Karen. "The Big Top & Beyond: Calder at the Whitney." *The New Criterion,* Vol. 10, No. 5, January 1992.

Zafran, Eric M. *Calder in Connecticut.* New York: Wadsworth Atheneum Museum of Art and Rizzoli International, 2000.

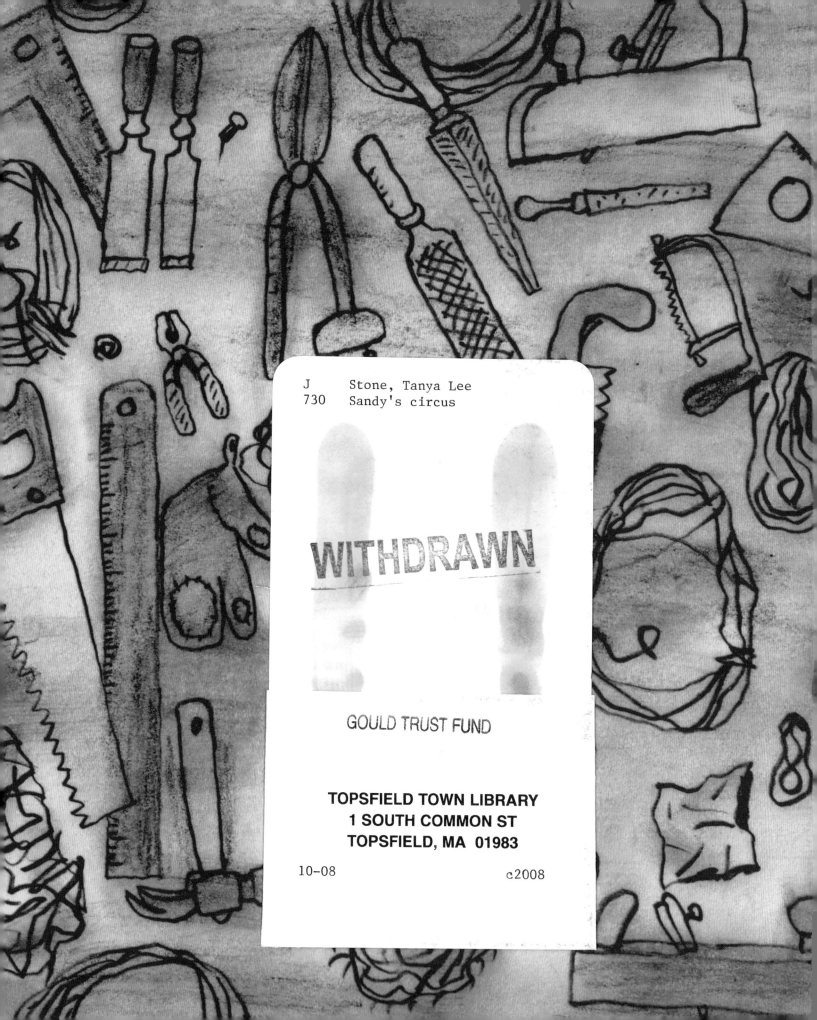